This Book Belongs To:

_____

Your Opinion Matters!

Did you know **84% of people rely on product reviews** when making a decision to buy a product online? Please help us by submitting a review.

1. Select "Your Amazon" on the upper right-hand side of your screen.
2. Click on "Your Orders" to find this order.
3. Select "Product Review".

Thank you so much in advance,

Today We Write

Made in the USA
Monee, IL
09 January 2024

51459176R00068